Oh For The Joy!
Forgiven and Free in Christ

by

Floyd Bland

Copyright © 2020 by Floyd Bland. All rights reserved. No part of this book may be reproduced, transmitted, or stored in any form except as permitted under U.S. copyright laws. Requests for permission should be addressed to info@notwm.org.

This book has been written for Christian inspirational purposes only. It is not intended to provide legal or clinical advice to replace the services of qualified professionals. No liability is assumed for loss or damage from its content since readers are to assume full responsibility for their own personal safety and well-being.

Some content is recreated from the author's memory and altered to maintain anonymity. Any resemblance to actual persons, entities, or locales is coincidental.

Scripture quotations marked (AKJV) are Scripture quotations taken from The Authorized (King James) Version. Rights in the Authorized Version in the United Kingdom are vested in the Crown. Reproduced by permission of the Crown's patentee, Cambridge University Press.

Scripture quotations marked (NKJV) are from the New King James Version®. Copyright © 1982 by Thomas Nelson. Used by permission. All rights reserved.

Scripture quotations marked (NIV) are from the Holy Bible, New International Version®, NIV®.

Copyright © 1973, 1978, 1984, 2011 by Biblica, Inc. ™ Used by permission of Zondervan. All rights reserved worldwide. www.zondervan.com The "NIV" and "New International Version" are trademarks registered in the United States Patent and Trademark Office by Biblica, Inc. ™

Scripture quotations marked (NLT) are taken from the Holy Bible, New Living Translation, copyright ©1996, 2004, 2007, 2013, 2015 by Tyndale House Foundation. Used by permission of Tyndale House Publishers, Inc., Carol Stream, Illinois 60188. All rights reserved.

Some of the images used in this book are officially licensed from ©Graphics Factory.com.

ISBN-13: 978-1-7325342-1-6
Library of Congress Control Number: 2020911300

Looking to Jesus!

Table of Contents

With Gratitude viii

Introduction: Looking to Jesus..
    My Early Encounter 1
    Three Emerging Thoughts 7

Chapter One: Hitting the Jackpot...
    What a Haul 16
    Eternal Fortunes Lost 24
    Eternal Fortunes Recovered 28
    The Joy of the Lord 32

Chapter Two: In Christ, We Have Eternal Forgiveness ....
    Our Sin Nature vs God's Righteousness 42
    Forgiven with a New Identity 45
    In the Hands of God 52

Chapter Three: In Christ, We Have Eternal Freedom ....
    What is Freedom? 57
    Walking in Liberty 64
    Peace and Promises of God 72

Chapter Four: For the Joy Set Before Him...............................
    When the Dust Settles 77
    Navigating the Backside of the Mountain 80

Epilogue: Who Will Tell His Story? ....
    Tell it Right! 95

About the Author 102

With Gratitude

For God the Father, Jesus Christ the Son, and the Holy Spirit, I am grateful for Your love, grace, and mercy, which allow me to experience the ultimate joy associated with eternal forgiveness and freedom.

For my godly parents, loving wife, and supportive family, I am grateful for your interventions in my life that shaped me into who I am today.

For those unsung heroes and heroines, I am grateful for your prayers, encouragement, and assistance over the years.

For Pam Lagomarsino of Above the Pages Editorial Services and Paramita Bhattacharjee of Creative Paramita Book Cover Designs, I am grateful for your professionalism and expertise rendered to prepare this book for publication.

Introduction

Introduction
Looking to Jesus

My Early Encounter

As I look back, I believe it was during Sunday  school when I was first introduced to Hebrews 12:1–2 more than a half-century ago. However, before I elaborate further, let me provide some history and context.

To begin with, the Lord blessed me with Christian parents who loved and honored Him enough to practice a consistent Christ-likeness before me—although imperfect at times, as with us all—but consistent nonetheless.

They expressed love for their children not by merely telling us about the Lord Jesus Christ, but also by leading us to church, as a family, every Sunday also. Their actions spoke volumes.

Their faith and fidelity helped cultivate my desire to experience and learn about the awesome God they were showing and telling me consistently.

I should also note they were my good friends as well. So in retrospect, no one should ever trivialize the essential role that loving, nurturing, godly parents play in raising children in the right path, so that and when they are older, they will not leave it as Proverbs 22:6 (NIV) teaches. Others also share this view,

> There is no denying that culture and church play a major role in the developmental life of any person. But the role parents play in their children's lives far outweighs any other influence. What parents believe and how they live out their beliefs (positively or negatively) has a huge impact on their children.[1]

In our fast-paced, twenty-first-century world, little consideration is given to the sound, biblical parenting I received as a child. With absentee fathers and mothers, single-parent homes, blended families, and latchkey kids, no wonder so many children today are growing up with limited spiritual understanding.

Certainly, culture plays a significant role in our upbringing. Yet, I attribute so much more of my particular spiritual journey to the combined efforts of three extraordinary people who introduced me to the Lord Jesus Christ and helped me to understand abundant Kingdom living.

Dad, Mom, and Grandma were the perfect parents for me. They encouraged and supported my spiritual growth by taking the time to explain fundamental biblical truths in a way I could understand and adopt as my own life principles to practice consistently, just as they did, as these authors observe,

It's not enough to just provide materially for our children. It's the sole duty and highest responsibility for parents to cultivate spiritual truths in their children's lives as well.[2]

They were not alone in my development process. The Lord blessed us to join a church where there were many spiritually mature, biblically astute men and women who recognized the importance of quality, Bible-based Christian education and discipleship.

Thus, it was not by accident that our church members (and guests) were exposed to sound biblical teaching and training primarily through Sunday school, Sunday general worship, and the Sunday evening Baptist Training Union (or BTU).

Our church had a strong core of visionary and stable leaders, who facilitated a number of training and service opportunities for church members seven-days-a-week.

Those of us who availed ourselves regularly to these opportunities learned how to develop our spiritual gifts and secular abilities through church leadership, church administration, music ministries, greeting and hospitality, community outreach, community food and shelter programs, prison ministries, and other Christian service opportunities under the tutelage of capable, mature, knowledgeable, and dedicated mentors.

In addition, we were blessed to have astute Bible teachers, both men and women, who were adroit at facilitating the student's comprehension and incorporation of sound, fundamental scriptural nuances and doctrine critical for our spiritual development.

These teachers taught directly from the Bible, used supplemental materials, or they relied on "lesson quarterlies"[3] to lead us in our regular learning exercises and discussions.

It is also worth noting that my church experience is not an isolated one, for many today lived during that particular era and had a similar Christian experience.

These experiences are unlike today, where selfish indifference and self-centeredness seem to be the accepted norm. At that time, it was common—and expected—to find mature Christian "surrogate parents" within our churches and communities.

These wonderful men and women were our extended family, providing the care, guidance, discipline, and counsel we needed to grow into honest, hard-working, responsible, law-abiding, productive members of society.

The Lord used all these influences to help nurture a Christian faith and character that resonates in me today.

In particular, I was especially captivated by the solemn reverence they had toward God and His Word, along with the fervor, anticipation, and vigilance about our Lord's imminent return.

Again, no one is perfect, but I saw little hypocrisy. Thus, the more time I spent with them and listened to their personal faith stories, and observed their Christian conduct, the more they validated those wonderful faith stories for me.

This prompted me to learn more about the Lord for myself (and the more I learned about Him, the more I found their testimonies to be true, prompting me to learn even more about Him).

Ultimately, the Lord used all these influences to ignite a spark in me that changed my life forever. Over time, it became clear that the Lord was preparing me for life-long service.

Thus, one should never trivialize a church's need for quality, Bible-based Christian education and discipleship programs—*for all ages.* For it produces lasting, positive effects on church members as well as the surrounding community,

> So while effective Christian education isn't the only thing that matters in church life, it is by far the most influential factor in nourishing faith...congregations should be primarily about the task of "equipping saints" for ministry. The church structure and institution should empower people

for ministry, rather than accomplishing the ministry for them.[4]

This author further observes,

> The challenge to congregations, then, is to help each member see himself or herself as an active minister—as a representative of Christ in the world. When local churches take seriously this responsibility to nurture each person's faith, the work of the church will be done through and by its members, who are, after all, the church.[5]

As I served actively in my church and community, I wanted to serve more, especially as I considered the prospects of sure heavenly rewards,

> Lay not up for yourselves treasures upon earth, where moth and rust doth corrupt, and where thieves break through and steal: but lay up for yourselves treasures in heaven, where neither moth nor rust doth corrupt, and where thieves do not break through nor steal: For where your treasure is, there will your heart be also (Matthew 6:19–21 AKJV).

As time progressed, the Lord revealed His calling on my life: to become a husband and father, a college (later seminary) graduate, an ordained minister, an administrator, and a prison chaplain.

In Sunday school, we were encouraged to read aloud the Bible verses printed in the quarterly, assisting slow readers. After reading, the teacher led our discussions on the Scripture passages until we completed the lesson.

The Authorized King James Version was used primarily in our home devotions and church studies. Despite its dated English language, I learned to read, study, memorize, and grow fond of it over time.

This was how Hebrews 12:1–2 (AKJV) appeared to me on that particular Sunday morning (*my emphasis*):

> Wherefore seeing we also are compassed about with so great a cloud of witnesses, let us lay aside every weight, and the sin which doth so easily beset us, and let us run with patience the race that is set before us, Looking unto Jesus the author and finisher of our faith; who *for the joy* that was set before him endured the cross, despising the shame, and is set down at the right hand of the throne of God.

After reading the lesson, three thoughts emerged that still resonate within me today.

Three Emerging Thoughts

1) We are surrounded by a "great cloud of witnesses," which implies our physical death is

not the end of our existence. God gave us a spiritual dimension that will continue to live long after our bodies have passed away. (God also gives us the responsibility to choose where we spend our eternity in Heaven or Hell.)

In other words, along with the "Roll Call of Faith" of Hebrews 11:4–40, all those who have died in Christ surround us like a crowd of ardent spectators cheering us toward the successful completion of our individual Christian races. Just think. We have our own "cheering section" rooting for us!

In my case, Dad, Mom, and Grandma became part of the "great cloud of witnesses" when they passed away years ago. They are absent from the body and present with the Lord (2 Corinthians 5:8), awaiting His glorious return for us. Then they, along with all those who have "died in the Lord," will accompany Him to be reunited with us who are yet alive (1 Thessalonians 4:13–18).

I am comforted knowing that one day, very soon I will see Jesus along with all those precious saints, including my parents and extended family, "coming in the clouds with great power and glory" (Mark 13:26). A most welcome and most wonderful day that will be indeed. *Amen!*

2) We Christians are to make every effort to "lay aside" the continual practice of sin, particularly the ones we find extremely tantalizing and are within easy reach. Instead, we are to pursue

earnestly and heartily His righteousness consistently.

Jesus makes this observation (*my emphasis*) in Luke 11:35–36 (NKJV):

> Therefore take heed that the light which is in you is not darkness. If then your whole body is full of light, *having no part dark*, the whole body will be full of light.

"No part dark" means our lives are faith-driven, Spirit-powered, Christ-centered, and God-honoring quests for spiritual and moral purity publicly and privately, with no "secret" sins.

We strive to be the same spiritual and moral person, whether we are alone or in the company of others. In other words, what we do, and how we act on Sunday during church services should be the same way we act on Monday at home, work, or school.

The "what I do in the privacy of my own home" should never be shameful or embarrassing if ever disclosed publically, since our lives reflect an integrated, consistent ethic that flows from our genuine conversion in Christ,

> Sin is turning away from God. As someone has said, it is aversion from God and conversion to the world; and true repentance means conversion to God and aversion to the world. When there is true

contrition, the heart is broken for sin; when there is true conversion, the heart is broken from sin. We leave the old life, we are translated out of the kingdom of darkness unto the kingdom of light.[6]

In Jesus' *Intercessory Prayer* in John 17, He foretells how His followers live "in the world," yet they will never become "of the world" (John 17:15–18). This remains true for us today.

Our "spiritual eyes" must remain focused on the Lord Jesus Christ, who is the source and consummation of our faith in God, as His Spirit actively works within us.

Thus from the moment we meet Christ onward, ours is a life-long race where His penetrating words ring true for us each day,

> If any of you wants to be my follower, you must give up your own way, take up your cross daily, and follow me (Luke 9:23 NLT).

God commands us to be holy, just as He is holy (Leviticus 20:26). Jesus calls us to be perfect as God is perfect (Matthew 5:48). Jesus is the Vine, and as His branches, we can yield His fruit consistently, just as He states in John 15:5.

Although only Jesus was perfect, yet we can make every effort to refrain from habitual sin and let our lights shine before the world. Then we can glorify

God and be a blessing to others just as the Lord teaches in Matthew 5:16.

Unfortunately, dishonesty, deceit, and debauchery have become commonplace for many professing Christians as three-quarters of Americans identify themselves as Christian, yet only 13 percent say they have no faith at all. Only one in every four is Bible-minded, although nearly two-thirds have an orthodox view of God.[7]

Oh, how I long for a time when noble character with principled behavior is deemed as innate *Christian* characteristics.

To the modern-day society, inconsistent conduct has hampered our noble Christian witness,

> Christianity is often not portrayed well in media. It is not "politically correct" to be a Christian anymore. Social pressure to "fit in" as a Christian is largely absent. In contrast, it is considered more socially acceptable to embrace non-Christian identities and lifestyles that stand in conflict with biblical values.[8]

God's eternal purpose for His people—to do justly, love mercy, and walk humbly before Him each day—has not changed (Micah 6:8).

Jesus declared that as the Light of the World, His followers will not walk in darkness but will have the light of life instead (John 8:12). In this way, He affirms His righteousness and ours.

Christian faith changes human lives as we enter into the presence of the Living God. Drastically changed human lives think, speak, and act in ways that improve the welfare of others without being motivated by race, gender, culture, social status, or political affiliation. Such is our destiny,

> We don't have to be victims of our glands. We are not automations or victims. We are free to make choices, whether noble or ignoble. To live for money, power, or pleasure is to die one day and leave it all behind. Indeed, to live for anything except Christ will mean reaching the end haunted by guilt and despair.[9]

Contrary to popular belief, I yet believe that we as Christians can and do change the world around us for the better—one person at a time.

3) Jesus paid the price for our sin so that we can share in the perfect joy that was set before Him.

It is His most exhilarating joy that captivates our hearts and minds today and always as we receive His unfathomably precious gifts of forgiveness and freedom.

Over the next few pages, we will explore this third idea in greater detail. I believe that our understanding of the "joy" set before Him, produces an assurance, comfort, and security we will not find anywhere else on earth.

Before we explore the next chapter, I will present an enduring hymn that encapsulates the blessed joy and assurance we have in knowing Christ.

Blessed Assurance[10]
Fanny J. Crosby
(1820—1915)

Blessed assurance, Jesus is mine! Oh, what a foretaste of glory divine! Heir of salvation, purchase of God, Born of His Spirit, washed in His blood.

Perfect submission, perfect delight, Visions of rapture now burst on my sight; Angels descending, bring from above Echoes of mercy, whispers of love.

Perfect submission, all is at rest, I in my Savior am happy and blest; Watching and waiting, looking above, Filled with His goodness, lost in His love.

Chorus:
This is my story; this is my song, Praising my Savior all the day long; This is my story, this is my song, Praising my Savior all the day long.

Notes

[1] Alex McFarland and Jason Jimenez, *Abandoned Faith: Why Millennials are Walking Away and How You Can Lead Them Home*, (Carol Stream: Tyndale House, 2017), 31.

[2] McFarland and Jimenez, 226.

[3] Our lesson "quarterlies" were issued once per quarter (or every three months).

[4] Eugene C. Roehlkepartain, *The Teaching Church, Moving Christian Education to Center Stage*, (Nashville: Abingdon Press, 1993) 26.

[5] Eugene C. Roehlkepartain, 27.

[6] Dwight L. Moody, *The Overcoming Life*, Moody Classic Edition, (Chicago: Moody Press, 1995) 51.

[7] Bible-minded means reading the Bible during the past week and asserting its accuracy in the principles it teaches. See: The Barna Group, *Barna Trends 2018, What's New and What's Next at the Intersection of Faith and Culture*, (Grand Rapids: Baker, 2017) 210–211.

[8] McFarland and Jimenez, 61.

[9] Ted W. Engstrom and Norman B Rohrer, *Making the Right Choices, Maintaining Your Integrity in a World of Compromise*, (Nashville: Thomas Nelson Publishers, 1993) 154.

[10] Fanny J. Crosby, "Blessed Assurance," *Voice of Praise*, B.B. McKinney, ed., 12th ed., (Nashville: Broadman Press, 1947) 3.

Chapter One

Chapter One
Hitting the Jackpot

What a Haul

Imagine living where there was no death, pain, sickness, poverty, or sorrow. Here, everyone's spiritual, physical, emotional, and psychological needs are met with complete satisfaction.

Here, there are no financing or resource shortages and no housing or food shortages either. Even our deepest heart's desires are satisfied, just as if everyone wins the 250 million dollar lottery—*every day!*

In this world, perfect peace, innocence, tranquility, and safety abound. We thrive in the company of loving, supporting companions with the freedom to do anything and everything we want every moment, every day, for our entire lives.

People here are different also. They are completely altruistic and perfectly content, never obsessing over personal power, prestige, wealth, social advantage, petty agendas, or political gain.

Instead, they seek the physical, social, emotional, and spiritual welfare of everyone living around them with substantive, meaningful, benevolence.

Such is not the case in today's world. As the time just before writing this book, it seemed the entire world was paralyzed by fear and panic associated with the COVID-19 virus.

Before the pandemic, we had little restrictions on our social activities and travel. Our houses of worship, private sector industries, and public sector governments were functioning normally, and our recreation and sporting events were in full swing as well.

Then came the "shelter in place" mandate to reduce human contact and mitigate the spread of the virus. Wide-scale panic ensued, which exposed the selfishness and greed that jeopardized the health and safety of the sick and aged—those most susceptible to COVID-19 fatality.

Personal protective equipment (i.e., masks, gloves, and hand sanitizers, etc.), disappeared from store shelves almost immediately as people began hoarding for personal consumption, and monetary gain.

The same could be said for paper towels, toilet tissue, disposable wipes, and disinfectant sprays to the detriment of that same at-risk demographic. (While some of these items are slowly returning to store shelves, some online purchases require up to thirty days for delivery.)

Also, reports of online item sales at exorbitant prices reveal our lack of concern for our neighbor's safety. They also show how we want "what's best for me" at my neighbor's expense.

Conversely, in that "perfect" place we explored earlier, there is no selfishness, depression, doubt, fear, worry, or stress because God is always present.

Each moment of the day, we experience His gentle, loving presence, without the anxieties and fears associated with a destructive and counterproductive disposition,

> God can be known in personal experience. A loving Personality dominates the Bible, walking among the trees of the garden and breathing fragrance over every scene. Always a living Person is present, speaking, pleading, loving, working, and manifesting Himself whenever and wherever His people have the receptivity necessary to receive the manifestation.[1]

An impossible world, you say. Not really.

Such was the case when God created Adam and Eve and placed them in the Garden of Eden with everything they could ever want or need forever.

Let's pause for a moment to explore the actions of the loving Creator Genesis 1:1 (AKJV) depicts,

> In the beginning, God created the heavens and the earth.

This foundational passage of Scripture does not defend the existence of God. It merely presents a personal God, who is a loving, caring Creator and Sustainer of everything that has or will ever exist.

Words cannot describe the vastness of God sufficiently. Yet, one author gives his impression,

> Good Being, a fountain of infinite benevolence and beneficence towards his creatures. The Being whose purposes and actions spring from Himself, without foreign motive or influence: he who is absolute in dominion; the most pure, the most simple, and most spiritual of all essences; infinitely benevolent, beneficent, true, and holy: the cause of all being, the upholder of all things; infinitely happy, because infinitely perfect; and eternally self-sufficient, needing nothing that he has made: illimitable in His immensity, inconceivable in His mode of existence, and indescribable in His essence; known fully only to Himself, because an infinite mind can be fully apprehended only by itself. In a word, a Being who, from His infinite wisdom, cannot err or be deceived; and who, from His infinite goodness, can do nothing but what is eternally just, right, and kind.[2]

Could not such a Being create all that exists today? Could He not also preserve and sustain it? God continues to do all these things and more as Nehemiah 9:6 (NLT) tells us,

> You alone are the LORD. You made the skies and the heavens and all the stars. You made the earth and the seas and everything in them. You preserve them all, and the angels of heaven worship you.

Instead of expressing Himself as an impersonal, ambiguous force to be reckoned with, God chooses to fellowship with the pinnacle of His creation, the human species.

God fixed our incomparable destiny forever in the Garden of Eden as we thrived in His loving, holy presence as He supplied our spiritual, physical, emotional, and psychological needs abundantly.

God designated human beings to be separate and distinct by creating us "in His image and likeness." As such, we can have loving, joyful, fulfilling, fellowship with Him forever. Genesis 1:26–27 (NLT) relates,

> Then God said, "Let us make human beings in our image, to be like us. They will reign over the fish in the sea, the birds in the sky, the livestock, all the wild animals on the earth, and the small animals that scurry along the ground." So God created human beings in his own image. In the image of God he created them; male and female he created them.

Our creation was most distinctive,

> It is clear that man, as God made him, was distinctly different from the animals already created. He stood on a much higher plateau, for God created him to be immortal, and made him a special image of His own eternity. Man was a creature with whom His maker could visit and have fellowship and communion. On the other hand, the Lord could expect man to answer him and be responsible to him. Man was constituted to have the privilege of choice, even to the point of disobeying his Creator. He was to be God's responsible representative and steward on the earth, to work out his Creator's will and fulfill the divine purpose.[3]

Through His creation, we see God's majesty and design to ensure our happiness and well-being in the most intricate detail. Thus, as Genesis 1:31 tells us, God's creation is "very good!"

Just think! The entire universe, with its galaxies, solar system, and our earth, including everything in the sky, underwater, and on land, was not created for eternal fellowship with God. Only you and I were created to fulfill this uniquely wonderful purpose.

People who do not see themselves as God's greatest creation sadden me. This is because He esteems you and I greater than Mount Everest, the Grand Canyon, Aurora Borealis, Victoria Falls, Table Mountain, the Barrier Reef, the Amazon Rainforest, the magnificent Redwoods, and all the sun, moon, and stars combined.

However, when we move to the opposite extreme, when our overactive sense of pride and self-importance seduce us into thinking we are the creator, and He is the created, then this becomes a real problem.

Here, we think we can "save our atmosphere," "control the climate," "prevent global warming," etc. when we are mere caretakers of His creation.

We are guilty of blasphemy. Because "saving," "controlling," and "preventing" far exceed our human capacity. Our actions are mere futile attempts to encroach on God's preservation and providence. Only God can preserve the earth and all that is in it,

> Preservation is that continuous agency of God by which He maintains in existence the things He has created, together with the properties and powers with which He has endowed them. Preservation implies a natural concurrence of God in all operations of matter and of mind. Without His concurrence, no person or force can continue to exist or to act.[4]

In six-thousand years of human history, I find it both profoundly preposterous and utterly arrogant to conceive the notion that our twenty-first-century generation can "save" anything.

I concede we have the technology our ancestors would have never imagined were possible. In addition, I do not contend conservation is worthless. I believe we should care for God's creation.

I do contend, however, even with our greatest human strength, we cannot control the earth's rotation, and we cannot stop the rain from falling. We cannot control the wind from blowing, and we cannot stop oceans from flowing either.

If everyone on our planet worked simultaneously for a million years, we still could not raise or lower our earth's temperature one degree, or otherwise control our environment—at will.

Our inability to "save" ourselves from COVID-19, other pestilence, earthquakes, floods, tropical storms, and the forces of nature should show us how frail and inadequate human strength really is.

It has always been, and it will always be God's job to "save" our planet and us—not ours.

Nevertheless, God gave us an amazing pedigree when He breathed in us His "breath of life" (Genesis 2:7), thereby purposely and deliberately imparting an everlasting human spirit within us.

The psalmist declares God designed us to be lower than the angels and crowned with glory and honor with all things under our feet (Psalm 8:5).

"In His image" also denotes our self-awareness, personality, and moral consciousness or holiness, which separates us from all the other creatures,

> Holiness, on the one hand, implies entire freedom from moral evil; and, upon the other, absolute moral perfection. Freedom from impurity is the primary idea of the word. To sanctify is to cleanse; to be holy, is to be clean.[5]

In the perfect world, we have pure and unlimited access to God. He knew us perfectly, and we knew Him perfectly, sharing in all phases except in those qualities that places Him above us as God (i.e., omniscience, omnipresence, omnipotence, eternity, self-existence, immensity, etc.).

Also, love, goodwill, benevolence and other noble traits are the norm. No one ridicules or criticizes us for practicing them.

Then tragedy struck and changed everything forever.

Eternal Fortunes Lost

Eternal bliss was ours with one caveat; do not eat the fruit from the Tree of the Knowledge of Good and Evil,

> The Lord God placed the man in the Garden of Eden to tend and watch over it. But the Lord God warned him, "You may freely eat the fruit of every tree in the garden—except the tree of the knowledge of good and evil. If you eat its fruit, you are sure to die" (Genesis 2:15–17 NLT).

When our ancestors ate the fruit, spiritual and physical death happened as God warned. Our physical death occurred over time, but our spiritual death was immediate, and it contaminated the entire world with sin.

Our eternal fellowship with God was lost forever leaving us with a sinful spiritual condition that causes us to think, speak, and act in sinful ways. By sin I mean,

> A lack of conformity to the moral law of God, either in act, disposition, or state.[6]

Through the transgressions of our ancestors, sin became our inheritance. As a result, we are inclined to practice it instead of seeking after godly things by nature as the Bible depicts,

- Behold, I was brought forth in iniquity, and in sin my mother conceived me. – Psalm 51:5 (NKJV)

- Indeed, there is no one on earth who is righteous, no one who does what is right and never sins. – Ecclesiastes 7:20 (NIV)

- The heart is deceitful above all things, and desperately wicked: who can know it? – Jeremiah 17:9 (AKJV)

- For all have sinned and fall short of the glory of God. – Romans 3:23 (NKJV)

- Therefore, just as through one man sin entered the world, and death through sin, and thus death spread to all men, because all sinned. – Romans 5:12 (NKJV)

- But the natural man does not receive the things of the Spirit of God, for they are foolishness to him; nor can he know them, because they are spiritually discerned. – 1 Corinthians 2:14 (NKJV)

Our evil deeds do not make us sinners. We are sinners (and do evil deeds) because of our sin contaminated spiritual nature in continual operation inside us.

When our massive fortune was lost, we exchanged our peace and harmony with God for discord and animosity. In other words, we've lost fellowship with God because He never fell from perfection. We did.

In addition, our sinful nature puts us in eternal jeopardy because His normal response to sin is judgment (wrath) and eternal separation.

By nature, we are the "children of wrath" (Ephesians 2:3), who are subject to God's judgment in a fiery Hell, separated from God. Jesus describes it as a real place where worms never die, and where tormenting fire burns forever (Mark 9:48).

Those of us who try to live a "good life" by doing good deeds might ask, "How can we be sinners? We are endowed with a moral compass reflected in our love, kindness, and benevolence toward other people. Right?"

Yes! We have the ability to perform good deeds. However, our sin nature skews our moral compass,

> There is a way that appears to be right, but in the end it leads to death (Proverbs 14:12 NIV).

Moreover, guilt, shame, depression, anxiety, doubt, worry and fear are some of the troubling byproducts of our sin nature "good people" indiscriminately suffer every day.

As fallen humans, we cannot do enough good to earn God's peace and favor, because He is the embodiment of justice and righteousness. His righteousness demands obedience to His moral perfection while His justice or wrath addresses our disobedience with wrath.

In our own strength, we are helpless and hopeless, always falling short. Here, the Bible rightly teaches, "It is a fearful thing to fall into the hands of the living God" (Hebrews 10:31 NKJV).

But thank God, this is not how our story has to end.

Eternal Fortunes Recovered

Romans 6:23 tells us the payment for sin is death. In short, someone had to die, and blood had to be shed to remediate our sin,

> For the life of the flesh is in the blood, and I have given it to you upon the altar to make atonement for your souls; for it is the blood that makes atonement for the soul (Leviticus 17:11 NKJV).

God gave Moses instructions on how animal blood would pay for our sins. However, this was not a permanent fix since people had to repeat it often.

Instead, it foreshadowed a God-given, restitution that would wash away our sins completely, make us righteous before God, and restore our lost fellowship forever.

God could have solved our sin problem by programming us to obey him like robots, but He wanted us to love Him freely and willingly.

He also could have overlooked our sin nature altogether. But, then He would have had to make Himself less than holy by sacrificing His righteousness for our unrighteousness.

As humans, we had no means to pay sin's price completely, so God chose the most effective remedy. He became human, in the person of Jesus Christ so that He could pay the price for our sin Himself,

> For God so loved the world that he gave his one and only Son, that whoever believes in him shall not perish but have eternal life. For God did not send his Son into the world to condemn the world, but to save the world through him (John 3:16–17 NIV).

Through Christ, we can have our eternal fortunes recovered and possess a new position and standing with God. Here, we must place our faith in Jesus as our personal Lord and Savior. Then, we become born again as His Holy Spirit comes into us to enliven our sin-deadened spirits forever.

Alive in Christ, our main objective now is to please Him each day. Only then can we fulfill our God-given, life purpose, to live abundantly as spiritually transformed and graciously redeemed children of God's glorious and eternal Kingdom.

Without considering our "good" works, God bestows Jesus' righteousness on us because of our faith in His sacrifice at Calvary,

> For by grace you have been saved through faith, and that not of yourselves; it is the gift of God, not of works, lest anyone should boast (Ephesians 2:8–9 NKJV).

It will never be possible for us to understand God's mysteries completely. He is infinite; we are finite. As the heavens are high above the earth, so are His ways and thoughts loftier than what we could ever think, hope, or imagine (Isaiah 55:9).

As our Sovereign Lord, God can conceal or disclose anything He chooses. Yet, He chose to reveal His divine, redemptive plan requiring only our simple faith in Christ to obtain it.

The Old Testament portrays God as One who judges the world in righteousness and promises to redeem all who turn to Him,

> Let all the world look to me for salvation! For I am God; there is no other (Isaiah 45:22 NLT).

However, in the New Testament, Jesus Christ is the One who bestows all judgment and redemption for us,

> Moreover, the Father judges no one, but has entrusted all judgment to the Son, that all may honor the Son just as they honor the Father. Whoever does not honor the Son does not honor the Father, who sent him (John 5:22–23 NIV).

Through Jesus Christ, our massive fortune is restored in the form of complete redemption and eternal reconciliation. Our new standing in Christ, or justification, expunges our sin record forever resulting in eternal life with God,

> Justification is a judicial or forensic act, i.e., an act of God as judge proceeding according to law, declaring that the sinner is just, i.e., that the law no longer condemns him, but acquits and pronounces him to be entitled to eternal life.[7]

We enjoy eternal peace and favor with God along with all the blessings we will ever need in this life and the next.

Just imagine for a moment. Eternal peace of mind is ours today! All our worries, anxieties, and fears are replaced with His intense feeling of calm, assurance, and ease because our minds are on the Lord,

> You will keep him in perfect peace, Whose mind is stayed on You, Because he trusts in You (Isaiah 26:3 NKJV).

Ours is a perfect peace that lasts forever. Jesus declares herein lies our source of great comfort,

> Blessed are they that mourn: for they shall be comforted (Matthew 5:4 AKJV).

It is our source of intensely wonderful joy as well.

The Joy of the Lord

In the Introduction, I relate how my extraordinary parents introduced me to the Lord Jesus Christ and helped to nurture me along my faith journey.

One of the greatest lessons they taught me was how my Creator and Redeemer established my identity two thousand years ago at Calvary's Cross.

His incomparable and indescribable act of love, grace, and mercy defines *who* and *Whose* I am forever.

Oh, the joy I felt, even as a child when I understood how special and unique I am because God loves me, and He gives me eternal forgiveness and freedom.

In other words (time to be selfish), He doesn't just love Noah, Abraham, Moses, Peter, Paul, and John. He loves me too. He died for me, He rose for me, He's preparing a place for me, and He's coming again soon for me!

What a Wonderful Savior!

From that time forward, the Angel of the Lord's "tidings of great joy" (Luke 2:10) took on a new, personal, and extremely riveting meaning.

In Romans 14:17, we live lives filled with righteousness, peace, and "joy" in the Holy Spirit. In Hebrews 12:2, we fix our spiritual gaze constantly upon Jesus Christ, who endured our suffering and death for the "joy" (of restoring a fallen humanity to a blessed, loving, eternal fellowship with God) set before Him.

The Greek word used for "joy" in each instance is *chara* (Strong-G5479), which conveys the idea of cheerfulness, calm delight, gladness, to be exceedingly joyful, or joyous.[8]

It is that most pleasurable, most satisfying, most delightful, ever-present state of being; powered, guided, and sustained by the Holy Spirit of God.

Now and forever, we fix our gaze on what the Lord has done for us, what He is now doing for us, and what He will do for us. This produces within us a pure, unbridled, and lasting joy,

> The delight of the mind arising from the consideration of a present, or assured possession of a future good...When joy has so long possessed the mind that it has settled into a temper[ment], we call it cheerfulness. This is natural joy.[9]

The Holy Spirit's activity is what distinguishes our joy from the giddiness linked to our capricious feelings, which can fluctuate at a moment's notice,

> From the witness of the spirit, Paul says, "We...rejoice in hope of the glory of God," because the love of God is shed abroad in our hearts, by the Holy Ghost given to us. That is, the Holy Ghost assures us that we are the objects of that love which he goes on to describe as infinite, immutable, and gratuitous. (Romans 5:3-5) And again, "The Spirit itself beareth witness with our spirit that we are the children of God." If, therefore, any true believer lacks the assurance of faith, the fault is in himself and not the plan of salvation, or in the promises of God.[10]

The Holy Spirit keeps our thoughts and desires on today's salvation and tomorrow's bliss while perfecting His joy within us simultaneously. Here, He produces His reassuring fruit (joy) inside us as Galatians 5:22 teaches.

More than just our Comforter, who "seals" our redemption and secures our heavenly home. The

Holy Spirit gives us life, direction, purpose, and meaning.

He is the Almighty God in Spirit, fully capable of purifying, revealing, strengthening, encouraging, and keeping us throughout our life's journey.

Yet as our Comforter, He intensifies our joy each time He brings to mind those precious promises in the Bible that reveal how wonderful our God is.

One such enduring promise is Psalm 23 (NLT), where the Lord, our Good Shepherd faithfully watches over and provides for us,

> The LORD is my shepherd; I have all that I need. He lets me rest in green meadows; he leads me beside peaceful streams. He renews my strength. He guides me along right paths, bringing honor to his name. Even when I walk through the darkest valley, I will not be afraid, for you are close beside me. Your rod and your staff protect and comfort me. You prepare a feast for me in the presence of my enemies. You honor me by anointing my head with oil. My cup overflows with blessings. Surely your goodness and unfailing love will pursue me all the days of my life, and I will live in the house of the LORD forever.

I beg to differ with those who characterize the Christian faith as merely a "pie-in-the-sky" religion. To them, all we have is eternal bliss in Heaven and nothing to look forward to on earth.

This is not so. The Christian faith produces a life of abundance (John 10:10), which begins the moment we accept Jesus Christ as our Savior and Lord and it continues forever.

Just our peace of mind alone, makes the Christian life more valuable than anything else on earth, and it certainly makes life worth living "in real-time" today.

We who embrace the Christian journey have considerable treasures to gain in this life and the next,

> The incentive to win is in the glorious perspective we have because we are "looking unto Jesus." "Looking away from all else, looking at that which fills the heart." We are going to run, not because of the prize at the end and not because so many illustrious saints have run the course in the past and have been gloriously crowned, but because the vision of Jesus thrills the soul.[11]

Our joy is never temporary or whimsical. It is always at work within us—despite our circumstances—reminding us of God's vast love, mercy, and goodness toward us.

This joy of the Lord served me well during my formative years. As we never had much money, we had to live in public housing and low-income apartments until the Lord blessed us with our own home.

His joy sustained me through our lack of clothes and food, along with the disappointments I faced over the years.

One time in particular, Dad helped me build a model car we entered in a race where the fastest cars received awards. Dad and I were thrilled when my car won its heat—just before the unthinkable happened.

A judge disqualified my car and initiated a re-qualifying second race.

What I remember most about that day was not how my car lost that second race and the tournament as a result.

I remember seeing the helpless expression on my Dad's face when our eyes met. Without speaking, I knew we both felt violated and cheated due to an unmerited disqualification, along with a "fixed" second race.

The helplessness and disappointment I felt that day has been long forgotten and forgiven.

In retrospect, I do not recall seeing other people of color at this event (which occurred when racial segregation was a societal norm). So whether the disqualification was racially motivated or not, I will never know; frankly, I don't want to know.

Nevertheless, attempts to "redefine" my identity by the imposition of an arbitrary standard failed. Although some may consider me as a "minority" because of my skin color, I knew my Creator and Redeemer makes no distinction.

Moreover, the Lord God Almighty lives within me, and He sees *all* His Children—including me—through His loving and affirming eyes,

> Be strong and courageous. Do not be afraid; do not be discouraged, for the LORD your God will be with you wherever you go (Joshua 1:9 NIV).

Ultimately, the Lord reminded me that He uses our fleeting hardships to work out His most excellent, eternal glory, which far surpasses anything we will experience in this life (2 Corinthians 4:17).

Thus, the model car could never make me a winner—or a loser. For in Christ, I am and will always be a "winner!"

The Lord is my confidence, and through the years, His joy has been my strength (Nehemiah 8:10), especially in troubling and uncertain times.

The Bible warns we will face adversity in life (Job 14:1), but the LORD promises to rescue us (Psalm 34:19). Therefore, I have not been exempt from calamity, misfortune, sorrow, or loss. Yet, I have His sure and certain promise,

> Weeping may last through the night, but joy comes with the morning (Psalm 30:5 NLT).

God's temperament of joy has helped me trust in Him with all my heart and not rely on my intuition always acknowledging Him so He can always direct my steps perfectly (Proverbs 3:5–6).

In John 16:33, the Lord promises our good cheer since He overcame this world's worst, a cruel death on a Roman cross for the joy set before Him reserved in Heaven for all of us.

Even more amazing is how Jesus Christ, our Righteous Judge forgives our sins completely. In the next chapter, we will explore this further.

Notes

[1] A.W. Tozer, *The Pursuit of God*, 2nd ed., (Camp Hill: Wing Spread Publishers, 1993) 48.

[2] Adam Clarke, "Genesis," *The Holy Bible Containing the Old and New Testaments with a Commentary and Critical Notes*, Vol. 1, new ed., (Nashville: Abingdon Press, 1977) 27.

[3] Charles F. Pfeiffer, "Genesis," *The Wycliffe Bible Commentary*, Charles F. Pfeiffer and Everett F. Harrison, ed., 8th ed., (Chicago: Moody Press, 1972) 4.

[4] Augustus H. Strong, *Systematic Theology*, 31st ed., (Valley Forge: Judson, 1976) 410–411.

[5] Charles Hodge, *Systematic Theology*, 3rd printing, vol. 1, (Peabody: Hendrickson, 2003) 413.

[6] Augustus H. Strong, 549.

[7] Charles Hodge, vol. 3, 119.

[8] James Strong, "χαρά," "Dictionary of Greek Words," *Strong's Exhaustive Concordance of the Bible*, updated ed., 3rd printing, (Peabody: Hendrickson Publishers, 2009) 1683.

[9] Merrill F. Unger, "Joy," *Unger's Bible Dictionary*, 18th printing, (Chicago: Moody Press, 1972) 613.

[10] Charles Hodge, vol. 3, 107.

[11] John Phillips, *Exploring Hebrews, An Expository Commentary*, rev ed., (Grand Rapids: Kregel Publications, 1988) 176–177.

Chapter Two

Chapter Two
In Christ, We Have Eternal Forgiveness

Our Sin Nature vs God's Righteousness

In the last chapter, we explored how we are  created "in the image" of God. Our ancestors disobeyed God. This resulted in our physical deaths, which terminates human life, and created spiritual death that produces sinful conduct and alienation from God.

When we try to follow Old Testament Law to restore our lost fellowship with God, we discover it's merely a guide, and we experience its limitations and our futility (Galatians 3:24).

To its merit, its contents help us understand sin and righteousness from God's perspective. Also, its wonderful promises of peace and prosperity, help us know God's principles for proper worship, service, and love even today, just as Jesus predicts,

> I tell you the truth, until heaven and earth disappear, not even the smallest detail of God's law will disappear until its purpose is achieved (Matthew 5:18 NLT).

Achieving God's righteousness would be simple if we could keep the Law. But unfortunately, our nature prompts us to worship other gods, create idols, use God's name irreverently, break the Sabbath, disrespect our parents, commit murder, be sexually promiscuous, steal, lie, and covet.

Since the Ten Commandments are impossible to keep, we see clearly God never intended for the Law to make us righteous. Instead, it serves to remind us how condemned we are—since we cannot keep it.

What's more, with all the technology, self-help, and other resources we have at our disposal, our nature prevents any resolution to our sin problem.

We see the tragic futility of people who attempt to make restitution to God through wealth, sports, notoriety, political power, corporate achievement, social significance, academia, technology, and medicine on display in our global media,

> People everywhere invest their lives in the search for meaning, purpose, and fulfillment. They seek something more than money, fame, luxurious houses, good looks, nice cars, or a lucrative stock portfolio. Nothing is wrong with these things, but they cannot provide peace to the soul or forgiveness of one's sin...Where one stands with God is the most vital of all issues, but the good news is that you may settle this today![1]

Although by nature, we are unfit to spend eternity in a glorious Heaven, we are well suited to spend eternity in a tormenting Hell separated from God.

I've spent considerable time helping prepare individuals for societal reintegration after they've completed their prison sentences. Yet, I have noticed strong public resistance against them.

Perhaps our resistance is from the fear they will vandalize our property, steal from us, assault a family member or friend, or commit some crime.

It occurs to me that if we can be so sensitive about living around undesirables, should we not expect our holy God to be sensitive about undesirables having access to His holy Heaven?

First Corinthians 6:9 (NKJV) asks, "Do you not know that the unrighteous will not inherit the kingdom of God?" It should not surprise us God has a "no sinner allowed" policy that remains in force today.

We are powerless to fix our condition using external, physical methods. Thus, intimacy with God is impossible without clean hands and a pure heart,

> Who may ascend the mountain of the LORD? Who may stand in his holy place? The one who has clean hands and a pure heart, who does not trust in an idol or swear by a false god. They will receive

blessing from the LORD and vindication from God their Savior (Psalm 24:3–5 NIV).

Forgiven with a New Identity

Earlier, we explored how the payment for our sin is death and how Jesus Christ had to die, and shed His blood to remediate our sin. In Matthew chapter 9:6, He declares, as the Son of Man, He has been given the authority to forgive our sins.

Until that time, forgiveness of sin was reserved for God in Heaven only. Now, Jesus insists that as God's *Suffering Servant* (Isaiah 53), He forgives our sin—past, present, and future. However, we *must* accept His invitation--freely and willingly,

> Look! I stand at the door and knock. If you hear my voice and open the door, I will come in, and we will share a meal together as friends (Revelation 3:20 NLT).

Jesus could do this because, He was 100 percent human, yet He satisfied all the statutes of the Old Testament Law, and He offered Himself as our complete, permanent sacrifice for sin.

Jesus Christ is not just our Prophet, whose life and teaching give us moral and spiritual direction. Nor is He merely our King, who governs our hearts and minds through His Holy Spirit.

He is also our Great High Priest, in whom we have the complete forgiveness of our sin forever,

> But Christ came as High Priest of the good things to come...Not with the blood of goats and calves, but with His own blood He entered the Most Holy Place once for all, having obtained eternal redemption (Hebrews 9:11–12 NKJV).

Jesus' perfect sacrifice covers our sin as the Lamb of God (John 1:29), who is fully capable to save "to the uttermost" all who come to God by Him, seeing He lives forever to make intercession for us (Hebrews 7:25).

Forgiveness of sin alone leaves us deficient before our holy God. His righteousness must be satisfied also,

> If God merely declared us to be forgiven from our sins, that would not solve our problems entirely, for it would only make us morally neutral before God. Such a movement is not enough to earn us favor with God. We must rather move from a point of moral neutrality to a point of having a positive righteousness before God, the righteousness of a life of perfect obedience to him.[2]

Made in God's image here involves our personal responsibility to choose. We can accept His gift of forgiveness and receive its blessings, or we can reject it and become subject to God's fierce wrath.

The moment we repent by turning from our sin and turning to God by faith in Christ, God cancels our sin debt and restores our fellowship instantly,

> Yet to all who did receive him, to those who believed in His name, He gave the right to become children of God—children born not of natural descent, nor of human decision or a husband's will, but born of God (John 1:12–13 NIV).

Through the blood of Jesus Christ, we can approach God *expecting* His acceptance as He exchanges Jesus' perfect life for our imperfect one. Now when He looks at us, He no longer sees vile sinners. He sees the "clean hands and the pure heart" of His Son, Jesus Christ the Righteous One. We are now suitable for His eternal fellowship.

Much like condemned criminals, we stand before the Righteous Judge, as guilty condemned, helpless, and hopeless because of our nature and our sins. Yet, His Son intercedes by assuming our sin, guilt, and penalty, and we receive His innocence, righteousness, and glory,

> The death penalty that Christ endured holds good for the believer, through his identification with Christ in His death; having been crucified as to his unregenerate nature, and justified from sin, he walks in newness of life in Christ.[3]

Instead of sentencing us to death, the Judge releases us with a new destiny. Now, with no troubling past, we are all the more aware that we matter to God.

Let's not overlook the fact that Jesus Christ possesses *all* power, in Heaven and in earth (Matthew 28:18)—*to forgive our sins*.

The Greek word used for forgive is *aphiemi* (Strong-G863), which means to let go, send away, to cancel, or to pardon.[4]

Thus in Christ, our sin nature is canceled, let go, sent away, pardoned, and forgotten forever. In fact, our sins no longer define us. Instead, God defines us by His great salvation,

> Through his life, death, resurrection, and exaltation, come deliverance from the guilt and power of sin and the gift of new life through the indwelling Holy Spirit. So the believer is saved by Christ's work on the cross (Acts 4:12); he is being saved now by the work of the Holy Spirit, the Sanctifier (Philippians 2:12) and he looks forward to completed salvation in the life of the age to come (1 Thessalonians 5:9, 1 Peter 1:5).[5]

God also looks beyond our past to extend His mercy to us—a people in need of restoration. Much like in the parable of the *Prodigal Son* (Luke

15:11–32), our Father no longer sees us as "dead and lost." He sees us as "alive and found."

It is our normal human reaction to demand retribution or keep mental and emotional records of wrongs when other people have offended us. But, God does not.

Although our fallen nature and sin offends Him far more than we could ever offend another person (we've disobeyed or ignored His perfect righteousness for us) yet, He keeps no record of our past. Neither does He impose a probation period until we "earn" His good graces. Psalm 103:12 tells us, He has removed our sins as far as the east is separated from the west.

Prompted by His great love, God restores us to full access to His Kingdom without restriction. In 1 John 4:10, love is defined by how God loved us enough to send His Son to be the payment for our sin. The Lord also directs our steps and takes special delight in every detail of our lives.

Liberated from our sinful past, our guilt and shame no longer confine us. Because nothing can separate us from God, nor can anyone or anything make us guilty before God,

> If God is for us, who can ever be against us?...Who dares accuse us whom God has chosen for his own? No one—for God himself has given us right standing with himself...Who then will condemn us? No

one—for Christ Jesus died for us and was raised to life for us, and he is sitting in the place of honor at God's right hand, pleading for us. Can anything ever separate us from Christ's love?...No, despite all these things, overwhelming victory is ours through Christ, who loved us. And I am convinced that nothing can ever separate us from God's love. Neither death nor life, neither angels nor demons, neither our fears for today nor our worries about tomorrow—not even the powers of hell can separate us from God's love. No power in the sky above or in the earth below—indeed, nothing in all creation will ever be able to separate us from the love of God that is revealed in Christ Jesus our Lord (Romans 8:31, 33-35, 37–39 NLT).

It is Satan's (or the Devil's) job to confuse and distort God's Word, by telling us we are utterly worthless. Unfortunately, his plan seems to have worked for those of us who feel we are "ugly" or "flawed," "will never amount to anything" and will be "worthless failures" in this life. These are lies, from the "pit of Hell."

Also, we should never obsess over being like other people since no two of us are exactly alike. It's ok for us to emulate another person, but we can never "be" that person. God created us differently. Individually, we are like the pieces of a jigsaw puzzle that when assembled create a beautiful portrait of God's love, redemption, and glory.

Satan (*our Enemy*) can also manipulate our past memories to perpetuate our insecurity with the lie that we will never be forgiven. People who fall prey to this lie will often remark, "God won't forgive me...You don't know who I am or what I've done!"

We cannot change our dysfunctional past. What's been done has been done. We must let go of that caustic spiritual, emotional, and psychological baggage to accept and embrace our new identity in Christ.

Besides, God knows us better than we know ourselves. He knows those "secret" sins few people if any know about. However, if He is willing to love, accept, treasure, value, and forgive us, then should we not be also willing to love, accept, treasure, value, and forgive ourselves?[6]

The massive weight of sin, guilt, and shame we've carried is finally gone. Now, we can forgive ourselves for our past blunders and function as completely forgiven children of God. When those troubling thoughts resurface to remind us of our sinful past, we can remind ourselves the blood of Jesus covers us; *we have been made brand new!*

Much like in John 8:1–11, we were brought before Jesus, helplessly condemned by accusers, clamoring for just retribution. Eventually we find ourselves alone in the very presence of our forgiving Savior and Redeemer, who asks us, "Where are your accusers?" We reply, "They've gone." Then, all at once, He reassures us, "I don't condemn you either...*Go and sin no more!*"

We can also help others experience our restored fellowship with God by participating in His "ministry of reconciliation" (2 Corinthians 5:18). Here, we forgive and forget past offenses to foster an atmosphere of spiritual and emotional wholeness.

In other words, God has forgiven us, and His Spirit lives inside us. As we surrender to Him, He gives us the ability to forgive or reconcile others. We all win when we forgive and reconcile to the same degree Christ has.

Yet even more amazing is how wonderfully He keeps us.

In the Hands of God

Ultimately, Jesus Christ left glory, not because of what we could do for Him but because we needed Him to pay our sin debt at Calvary, and to give us His Holy Spirit to comfort, secure, guide, and sustain us throughout our earthly journey.

The Lord loves us more than we could ever comprehend. It is not our works but our faith in His works that restores and secures our eternal fellowship. We don't rely on our capricious will and finite human ability to hold on to Christ while facing life's uncertainties. Instead, we rely on His infinite power and providence. It's up to Him to hold on to us and renew us as we press forward,

> But those who trust in the LORD will find new strength. They will soar high on wings like eagles. They will run and not grow weary. They will walk and not faint (Isaiah 40:31 NLT).

Our endurance is more about the Lord's omnipotence and faithfulness than it is about our finiteness and inadequacy. Article Eleven of "The Perseverance of the Saints," within the *New Hampshire Confession* states,

> We believe the Scriptures teach that such as are truly regenerate, being born of the Spirit, will not utterly fall away and perish, but will endure to the end; that their persevering attachment to Christ is the grand mark which distinguishes them from superficial professors; that a special Providence watches over their welfare; and that they are kept by the power of God through faith unto salvation.[7]

We focus on Christ, our Good Shepherd, whose providence watches over us, and His power keeps us. We find hope, strength, and victory in Jesus Christ as we steadily progress through this life toward our glorious heavenly home.

No one but Jesus Christ loves us so deeply, gives of Himself so freely, and keeps us so completely throughout this life and into the next,

> The path of the righteous is like the morning sun, shining ever brighter till the full light of day (Proverbs 4:18 NIV).

Jesus Christ is more than mere "fire insurance" because He is the embodiment of all God's promises. He's got it, and He's got us as well. Thus, we trust Him always, because He delivered us from a life of sin and He presents us before God as forgiven and righteous,

> Now unto him that is able to keep you from falling, and to present you faultless before the presence of his glory with exceeding joy, To the only wise God our Saviour, be glory and majesty, dominion and power, both now and ever. Amen Jude 24–25 (AKJV).

Our eternal life is both certain and secure, and this further enhances our joy. Our faith begins and ends with Jesus Christ, who is our hope, peace, expectation, and great reward, now and forever (Jeremiah 9:24, 1 Corinthians 1:31).

Freedom in Christ and peace with God are two additional benefits we have received. We will explore these benefits further in the next chapter.

Notes

[1] Alex McFarland and Jason Jimenez, *Abandoned Faith: Why Millennials Are Walking Away and How You Can Lead Them Home*, (Carol Stream: Tyndale House, 2017), 243–244.

[2] Wayne Grudem, *Systematic Theology, An Introduction to Biblical Doctrine*, (Leicester, England: Inter-Varsity Press; Grand Rapids, Michigan: Zondervan Publishing House, 1994) 725.

[3] W.E. Vine, "Freedom," *Vine's Expository Dictionary of New Testament Words*, W.E. Vine, Merrill F. Unger, William White, Jr., *Vine's Dictionary of Biblical Words*, (Nashville: Thomas Nelson, 1985) 255.

[4] See: James Strong, "ἀφίημι," Dictionary of Greek Words, *Strong's Exhaustive Concordance of the Bible*, updated ed., 3rd printing, (Peabody: Hendrickson Publishers, 2009) 1612, and Walter Bauer, "ἀφίημι," *A Greek-English Lexicon of the New Testament and Other Early Christian Literature* F. Wilbur Gingrich and Frederick W. Danker, ed., 2nd rev. ed. (Chicago: University of Chicago Press, 1979) 125.

[5] J.D. Douglas, Walter A. Elwell, and Peter Toon, "Salvation," *The Concise Dictionary of the Christian Tradition, Doctrine, Liturgy, History*, (Grand Rapids: Zondervan, 1989) 335.

[6] Participation in a Christian recovery program in conjunction with a church discipleship ministry, under the watchful care of specially trained, certified professionals can help us develop the coping strategies that help us address our physical/emotional trauma and/or compulsive addiction disorders and give us the critical accountability and support components necessary to the recovery process.

[7] See: Edward T. Hiscox, *The Standard Manual for Baptist Churches* (Philadelphia: American Baptist Publication Society, 1951) 67, and J. Newton Brown, *A Baptist Church Manual*, 37th ed., (Valley Forge: Judson, 1983) 15.

Chapter Three

Chapter Three
In Christ, We Have Eternal Freedom

What Is Freedom?

When we think of the word "freedom," we conjure up notions of unlimited mobility or liberty someone or something has without imposition, hindrance, or restraint. Webster's[1] defines freedom as,

> Not subject to the control or domination of another, exempt, not bound, confined or detained, capable of moving or turning in any direction; to cause to be free, to relieve or rid of what restrains, confines, restricts, or embarrasses.

I contend, however, our human freedoms can provide some short-term gratification, but they are never redemptive. We will always suffer from indiscriminate exploitation and victimization anywhere at any time—due to the presence of sin in our world.

Consequently, I thank God for the civic and moral laws in place that guard against the wanton pursuit of personal freedom at the expense of everyone else's.

As I digress for a moment, I can remember when racial segregation deprived many U.S. citizens certain basic freedoms. During that era, we associated freedom with racial justice and equality. So as Dr. Martin Luther King, Jr., and others both black and white spoke of freedom, it stirred our hopes for a better tomorrow with access to places and things unavailable to us at that time,

> Our freedom was not won a century ago, it is not won today...Today the question is not whether we shall be free but by what course we will win.[2]

In the wake of Dr. King's assassination, our astronauts landed on the moon. The '60s were behind us, and the '70s became our long awaited moment to *realize "the Dream,"*[3] and to embark on our brave new world filled with love and peace—*together!*

However, as Psalm 118:8 relates, it is far better to place our confidence in the Lord than in fallible human beings, even when we are well-meaning.

Thus, the onset of personal and political materialism, greed, and opportunism, along with "high-profile" moral failures in leadership, scandals, and false promises, coupled with the proliferation of sex, drugs, gangs, senseless violence, and more victimization, which subsequently followed should not have surprised us.

Fast forward to 2020, and we seem to be reliving our past hopes for a brave new world. However, five things are profoundly clear in retrospect,

1. Creating more laws, delivering eloquent orations, and protesting/demonstrating will not make people love each other, especially when an adversarial relationship exists between them.

2. It is pointless for anyone to expect to obtain the respect or love from another person if he or she does not love or respect themselves (or their own race).

3. Evocative rhetoric will not change a person—whether black or white—when his or her heart is full of malice, hatred, or ill will. The malevolence within a person will eventually reveal itself with painfully tragic results.

4. As long as sin and hatred are parts of our normal, day-to-day world, we will never experience "Heaven" on earth.

5. Only Jesus Christ can transform the very worst of us into forgiven and free citizens of the Kingdom of God. Through Him, we can experience real, lasting peace, justice, and equality—now and forever.

Things have improved for many disadvantaged people who took advantage of the opportunities in education and commerce that became available.

Incidentally, the freedoms we share as Americans, which we often take for granted, were never intended as licenses to do what we want, when we want, to whomever we want willy-nilly.

The increases in disrespect, hostility, and violence where we should exercise understanding, civility, and courtesy trouble me as well. All of us are free to express our opinions appropriately (i.e., without endangering the health, safety, or welfare of others), without the fear of censorship.

As a civilized people, we are to exercise vigilance and a swift dispatch in our moral responsibility to extend consideration toward our fellow citizens,

> The freedom of God is exercised and illustrated in his government of his moral creatures. It has pleased God to create intelligences possessed of moral freedom and to make their ultimate destiny contingent upon the right use of their freedom.[4]

Human freedoms carry with them a sacred duty to preserve public civility, decency, and goodwill especially within our own families and communities.

We share the world with others, so it would behoove us to foster a congenial atmosphere, which is in everyone's best interests. Otherwise, there will be more anarchy, hostility, and senseless violence to jeopardize everyone's safety.

Nevertheless, human freedom alone will not provide true lasting peace and fulfillment. Relied on alone, it becomes much like a broken cistern,

> For my people have committed two evils; they have forsaken me the fountain of living waters, and hewed them out cisterns, broken cisterns, that can hold no water (Jeremiah 2:13 AKJV).

Earthly freedom does not address our spiritual being; to be truly free, we must consider our spiritual dimension as well.

> Seek God and discover Him and make Him a power in your life. Without Him all of our efforts turn to ashes and our sunrises into darkest nights. Without Him, life is meaningless drama with the decisive scenes missing. But with Him we are able to rise from the fatigue of despair to the buoyancy of hope. With Him we are able to rise from the midnight of desperation to the daybreak of joy. St. Augustine was right—we were made for God and we will be restless until we find rest in Him.[5]

Our Lord presents a more comprehensive view of freedom moving it far beyond mere civic change to encompass a transcending dimension,

> You will know the truth, and the truth will set you free...I tell you the truth, everyone who sins is a slave of sin. A slave is not a permanent member of the family, but a son is part of the family forever. So if the Son sets you free, you are truly free (John 8:32, 34–36 NLT).

Jesus Christ is the embodiment of truth by which we experience absolute freedom. No longer slaves to sin, we can become new creations with new desires that emerge from our new disposition (2 Corinthians 5:17).

The Greek word He uses for "free" is *eleutheros* (Strong-G1658), which conveys the idea of one being unrestrained; to go at pleasure; not enslaved; to be exempt from obligation or liability; to go where ever one pleases.[6]

Derivatives appear in Galatians 5:1 (NKJV), which present a very similar picture (*my emphasis*),

> Stand fast therefore in the *liberty* by which Christ has made us *free*, and do not be entangled again with a yoke of bondage.

True freedom emerges from our complete surrender to Christ. His Spirit within us keeps anyone or anything from binding us.

We are forgiven and free followers of Jesus Christ, called to foster and preserve a civil world with a consecrated, Christ-centered life,

> I am crucified with Christ: nevertheless I live; yet not I, but Christ liveth in me: and the life which I now live in the flesh I live by the faith of the Son of God, who loved me, and gave himself for me (Galatians 2:20 AKJV).

Free, but crucified with Christ may seem contradictory, but it is not. The Lord gives us complete, unlimited freedom—not to sin. In other words, we are "free" to choose the wholesome, godly things our old nature discouraged us from engaging.

Now, we are free to strive for spiritual maturity by saying no to sin, *Satan*, and self. Now, we say yes to fasting, praying, reading God's Word, becoming active in a local church, fellowshipping with other Christians, and using our spiritual gifts to serve our church and community,

> Freedom, a condition of absolute liberty from all outward constraint, is only attained when man attains fellowship with God (who is absolutely free) in the truth: when that prompts man to action which prompts God.[7]

Our freedom allows us to go places, and do things that honor the Lord, completely oblivious to our "old master's" urgings to resume a life of sin. *Herein lies true, everlasting freedom!*

Our Lord Jesus Christ can break the bonds of drug addiction, sexual addiction, greed, guilt, shame, and other compulsive addictive disorders when we surrender to Him—completely.

It is amazing to see former "slaves to sin" experience God's freedom as they look to Jesus,

> Freedom (intellectual, moral, and spiritual) is only attainable when we are set free from darkness, sin, ignorance, and superstition and we let the Light of the World shine on and in us.[8]

His purging will be painful, but it is absolutely necessary for our spiritual growth and moral well-being.

Ultimately, He frees us to walk in liberty so we can be transparent and authentic as we work, study, serve, give, laugh, cry, and have fun without causing harm.

Walking in Liberty

First Things

Walking in liberty begins by taking care of first things, or our personal spiritual development, by growing to know and love God for who He is and what He has done for us. Here, we spend quality time in fasting and prayer, along with reading, studying, and memorizing His Word.

In the Bible, prayer is often associated with fasting (e.g., Daniel 9:3, Matthew 17:21, Luke 2:37, Acts 14:23, and 1 Corinthians 7:5). However, we must exercise extreme caution and care when fasting to maintain our personal health requirements.[9]

No longer indifferent or ambivalent about our relationship with the Lord, we regularly spend time in personal devotions that require our planned, purposeful, and deliberate involvement.

Liberty produces a strong sense of reverence toward the Lord. Prompted by His Spirit, we crave deeper intimacy, desire to grow closer, and are willing to surrender all phases of our lives to Him.

Much like a compass needle that points north because of the magnetic forces, liberty leads us to Christ as He lives in and works through us each day.

When Moses was on Mt. Sinai communing with God and receiving His Law, he felt inspired to make this request,

> Let me know your ways so I may understand you more fully and continue to enjoy your favor (Exodus 33:13 NLT).

Then in verse 18, he makes a request, which God answered and changed his appearance drastically,

Show me your glory!

After his encounter with God, Moses' face was illuminated. The people saw it and were in awe.

Like Moses, we too must desire to see our Lord's glorious presence in every arena of our lives. Then, we can grasp "the breadth, and length, and depth, and height" of His love as He reflects His radiance in us and through us (Ephesians 3:18).

Our Lord is a life-changing Spirit whose incredible majesty and splendor compel us to revere Him with a sober view of His eternal being.

This enables us to pursue His moral and spiritual perfection with all sincerity and dedication, so we can truly come to know who He truly is—and who we truly are as well,

> Your identity is found totally in Him. You can't know yourself until you know Jesus the way you should. And you for sure can't love Jesus the way you should until you know Him the way you should.[10]

As we walk in liberty, we keep our word, speak the truth in love, and have spiritual, emotional, and psychological congruity to develop "in wisdom, stature, and favor with God" just as our Lord did (Luke 2:52).

We also pray for others regularly while displaying emotional security by not being envious, afraid, threatened, or intimidated by their status, abilities, accomplishments, or possessions.

We trust the Lord's infinite wisdom and providence, fully confident that He can bring to completion His perfect work in us until the day of Jesus Christ (Philippians 1:6).

There will be times when our old master, sin, will tempt us. Yet, we do not blame others or use flimsy excuses to escape our accountability.

Instead, we ask the Lord for help so that His Spirit can free us to an improved moral and spiritual posture. Then as we've offended others, we reconcile with God and the person(s) we've offended by repentance and restitution.

Liberty also mandates we practice self-care, by protecting, preserving, and strengthening our bodies through adequate rest, exercise, and diet. We also reduce unhealthy levels of stress, abstain from drug and alcohol abuse, and engage in activities that honor Christ to make a difference in our world.

Further, liberty is reflected in our faith and fidelity with spiritual eyes that look to Jesus Christ for help, protection, and comfort.

He gives us the ears to listen to His soothing voice over the maddening clamor around us. He also gives us humble and submissive hearts that reflect His love and kindness tangibly.

We have helping hands that demonstrate His care and mercy, and we have swift feet to readily support His agendas—not ours—as we share His love toward the unloved.

His Spirit prompts us to faithful service at home and church. We do not perform our works to earn our salvation. Instead, they spring from our love for the Lord and our gratitude for what He has done for us and in us, now that we are saved.

We serve sacrificially, with renewed minds that reveal we no longer conform to our fallen world's standards. Instead, we transform them and underscore His good, perfect, and well-pleasing will for us and others at home and church (Romans 12:1–2).

Second Things

Liberty in the home is seen as we lead our families to church; we pray together and play together. We also treat each member with care, rendering no harm.

All members are safe from sexual, physical, and emotional abuse as we treat each other with dignity and respect instead of objects of our gratification. With no cutting, insensitive, and insulting remarks, we offer comforting words and positive affirmations to encourage and support each other accordingly.

Husbands and fathers serve as a spiritual leader, using Christ's love as an example to love their wives even to the extent of offering their lives for them. We also share our faith stories regularly, giving love, time, and attention to each member. Liberty shows that chasing careers, wealth, possessions, and "toys" are not nearly as important as preserving family well-being.

Material things cannot replace caring and listening parents. Wives feel safe to respond to the husband's lead as they share the responsibility to maintain a home where the Lord reigns.

Here, parents act like parents, and children act like children. Parents provide care and nurturing, along with consistent, appropriate discipline as we model a safe, free, reliable, and sincere lifestyle before our children.

In this way, we can train our children about the grave consequences associated with wrong actions so that they know how to function safely, free, and effectively in our global society. As we help our children pursue constructive, godly things, we provide the encouragement and support they need to devote a lifetime of service to the Lord in whatever vocational field they pursue.

Before the "end of life" time arrives, there may be "role reversals" as children provide care for their incapacitated parents. By doing so, we fulfill God's command to honor our fathers and mothers (Exodus 2:12).

As the most intimate way to grow toward Christian maturity, God uses families to affect the world through our shared faith and liberty.

Liberty in the church enables us to reflect the Kingdom of God as we worship, hear, and learn God's Word, fellowship, serve, and observe His ordinances.

Leaders provide care, biblical instruction, as they help us identify and use our gifts and resources that honor the Lord. We are free to practice mutual submission as we emulate our Lord's humility before our church and the world.

Whether parishioners or guests, we celebrate our diversity and unity and show His church is impervious to the gates of Hell (Matthew 16:18).

Other Things

Liberty also affects the other things in our life, including school, work, learning, and community.

At school, it frees us to better ourselves through formal training. We are respectful, punctual, studious, and sociable. We do not cheat on exams, plagiarize another's work, steal or misuse equipment, while we refrain from binge drinking, hazing, exhibitionism, and sexual promiscuity. After completion, we take what we've learned into the world where we use it to enhance the lives of others.

In the workplace, our liberty frees us to be God's faithful stewards as reliable, responsible, subordinate, on-time, hard workers, avoiding petty squabbles, never defrauding or abusing company resources, and we follow instructions (except when the integrity of our faith and/or our Christian conduct is/are overtly challenged).

As team players, we celebrate the achievements of our colleagues and are positive even when we do not receive recognition.

In the community, we form and nurture meaningful relationships, advance the noble causes of others, and treat people with the respect and dignity they deserve regardless of race, class, or gender.

Romans 13 instructs us to obey the laws of the land by submitting to and praying for our civic leaders (even when they do not share our political views). It refrains us from seeking to "get even" as a self-appointed vigilante.

Ultimately, liberty applies to every area of our daily human interaction. We please the Lord and bless others, which are always both right and proper.

Peace and Promises of God

Earlier, we explored how our faith in Christ, we are reconciled to God. As a result, we have true and lasting peace with Him,

> Therefore, since we have been made right in God's sight by faith, we have peace with God because of what Jesus Christ our Lord has done for us. Because of our faith, Christ has brought us into this place of undeserved privilege where we now stand, and we confidently and joyfully look forward to sharing God's glory (Romans 5:1–2 NLT).

Jesus is the Prince of Peace (Isaiah 9:6) Whose Spirit inhabits our hearts forever to foster peace and goodwill toward others. Our liberty and peace with God are complete and eternal. We are longer at odds with Him since Jesus promises we will never be cast out (John 6:37). Being reconciled to God allows us to reconcile with others.

God's peace and favor change our being, identity, and destiny forever as our "clear conscience" opens new and exciting possibilities as change agents in a world seeking peace,

> [Peace with God] expresses the state of reconciliation (opposite to the state of condemnation, 8. 1), in the consequence of the removal of God's wrath and the

> satisfaction of His justice by the sacrifice of Christ, who is our Peace; Ephesians 2. 14–16…Sin is the source of all discord and war between man and God, and between man and man; and hence there can be no peace until this curse is removed. All other peace is an idle dream and illusion. Being at peace with God, we are at peace with ourselves and with our fellow-men.[11]

We now reflect our Creator's dignity as His peace enables us to refrain from harboring grudges or expressing ill will, and be at peace with others. Heartily, we give people a "clean slate" and treat them as precious cargo in the sight of God, just as He does for us each day.

As we walk in liberty, we can extend peace and seek social harmony toward all people anywhere, even those who may not like us or may have offended us.

Motivated by love, our Lord extended His peace and reconciliation in our best interest. Now He lives within us making us truly free. As we walk in liberty, He is working through us to extend His peace and reconciliation to others in their best interests—motivated by His love.

God created us as social creatures with distinct personalities and temperaments. As such, our peaceful demeanor enables us to function according to His design to bring Him honor. Our minds control our cognitive and anatomical functions. God wants us to use these functions for proper thoughts, feelings, and perceptions, so that we can be sound examples of His love and peace as Ephesians 4:1–6 (NIV) attests,

> I urge you to live a life worthy of the calling you have received. Be completely humble and gentle; be patient, bearing with one another in love. Make every effort to keep the unity of the Spirit through the bond of peace. There is one body and one Spirit, just as you were called to one hope when you were called; one Lord, one faith, one baptism; one God and Father of all, who is over all and through all and in all.

We can become God's crowning achievements of salvation on this earth. As His set-free peacemakers, He has supplied us with all we will ever need to serve consistently as unique components of His wonderful master plan.

Ultimately, we are the fine examples of pure optimal living. We walk in God's liberty, with total peace of mind, and with a completely clear conscience.

In this way, we prove to the world that when the Son makes us free, we are free indeed!

Notes

[1] *Merriam-Webster's New Collegiate Dictionary*, (1977), G. & C. Merriam Company, 457–458.

[2] Coretta Scott King, *The Words of Martin Luther King, Jr.*, 1st. ed., (NY: Newmarket Press, 1983) 53.

[3] The "Dream" refers to the "*I Have a Dream*" speech Dr. MLK, Jr. delivered during the March On Washington on August 28, 1963.

[4] Merrill F. Unger, "Freedom," *Unger's Bible Dictionary*, 18th printing, (Chicago: Moody Press, 1972) 380.

[5] Coretta Scott King, 64.

[6] Moreover, *eleutheros* metaphorically describes our freedom from the slavery of sin. See: Spiros Zodhiates, "ἐλεύθερος," *The Complete Word Study Dictionary: New Testament*, rev. ed., (Chattanooga: AMG International, 1993) 566–567, and James Strong, "ἐλεύθερος," 1623, and Walter Bauer, "ἐλεύθερος," 250.

[7] Marcus Dods, "The Gospel According to John," *The Expositor's Greek Testament*, W. Robertson Nicoll, ed., reprint, vol. 1, (Grand Rapids: Eerdmans, 1980) 776.

[8] Archibald Thomas Robertson, "The Fourth Gospel," *Word Pictures in the New Testament*, renewal, vol. 5, (Grand Rapids: Baker, 1960) 149.

[9] Consulting one's medical care professional for fasting guidelines before fasting is highly recommended.

[10] Tony Evans, *Returning To Your First Love, Putting God Back In First Place*, (Chicago: Moody Press, 1995) 187.

[11] J.P Lange, and F.R. Fay, "The Epistle of Paul to the Romans," *Commentary of the Holy Scriptures: Critical, Doctrinal and Homiletical*, J.F. Hurst, P. Schaff and M.B. Riddle, trans., 7th ed., vol. 10, (Grand Rapids: Zondervan, 1980) 160.

Chapter Four

Chapter Four
For The Joy Set Before Him

When the Dust Settles

Now we've reached the section I've struggled with writing since the beginning. For  how can I adequately capture the emotions, anxieties, fears, doubts, and worries that trouble us when our personal presuppositions (concerning God, the world around us, and ourselves) are in direct conflict with our understanding and expectations of what we think the Bible says?

I call these the uncertain moments "when the dust settles."

Initially, we have euphoric joy from knowing and experiencing God's love, redemption, forgiveness, freedom, and liberty, along with His everlasting peace. We are at our highest point; we belong to God, and He belongs to us. *All is very well!*

Then unexpectedly, adversity strikes in the form of the loss of a child, parent, or someone dear to us; our near-death experience or poor health; the loss of career and income; the loss of our property and/or possessions; the loss that occurs which is beyond our control.

In these troubling moments, many of us look for comfort from others dear to us. Some of us even will anesthetize our pain through drugs and alcohol.

Still, some of us cope by using distractions like becoming more involved at work, church, or community volunteer work. Others seek comfort though isolation and close ourselves from the world.

Not long before his coronation, David and his men were affected by the loss of their families and property. They cried until they had no more tears.

David found no relief in his confederates. They blamed him for their loss and spoke of stoning him to death.

Yet, God was there for David. He soon experienced God's amazing comfort as he "strengthened himself in the LORD his God" (1 Samuel 30:6).

Although it may be difficult to find our sanity during excruciating and painful moments, we won't find real comfort through external means.

We find true comfort within from that Friend who is closer than a brother, and from relying on Him for answers, security, and lasting comfort (Proverbs 18:24).

Job's poignant words ring true here, "Though he slay me, yet will I trust in him" (Job 13:15 AKJV). Despite his adversity, Job was able to keep his focus on what really matters,

> I know that my Redeemer lives, and he will stand upon the earth at last. And after my body has decayed, yet in my body I will see God! I will see him for myself, Yes, I will see him with my own eyes. I am overwhelmed at the thought (Job 19:25–27 NLT)!

What really matters is God is with us today, and He will continue to be with us always, especially during our most painful moments.

At times, it can be hard to distinguish whether we are culpable for our "dust settling" or not. Often, we lash out and blame God for our trouble,

> People ruin their lives by their own foolishness and then are angry at the LORD (Proverbs 19:3 NIV).

I too have blamed the Lord when the outcomes of situations did not meet my unrealistic expectations.

But, after a time of somber, honest, and objective thought and reflection, coupled with some well-timed biblical counseling, it became even clearer that my poor choices caused my unfortunate circumstances.

Navigating the Backside of the Mountain

Imagine how disgraced Moses must have felt while he was tending Jethro's flock on the backside of the mountain in the Sinai wilderness. He had been accustomed to all the pageantry and splendor of Ancient Egypt as Pharaoh's grandson before he killed an Egyptian and fled the country.

He was responsible for his current situation, having murdered the Egyptian. Thus, for forty years, this former prince had to wear the titles of "murderer," "fugitive," and "vagabond" with only Jethro's flock as the subjects of his kingdom.

But, his life was not over. God had an assignment for Moses that was beyond his wildest dreams. For when this dejected, humiliated former prince found the Holy One in the Sinai Desert, his life changed forever.

In an act of submission and surrender, Moses removed his shoes, and he covered his face. Then, he renounced his past, surrendered his present situation, and began a life of consecrated and illustrious service.

Incidentally, this same mountain would serve as a source of faith, hope, and promise for Moses and an entire nation.

Moreover, the forty years he spent tending Jethro's flock adequately prepared him to lead his nation from the tyranny and oppression associated with Egyptian slavery to the freedom and good fortunes associated with being God's Chosen People in the "Promised Land."

Consequently, through Moses, we have the ceremonial and judicial principles that influence the religious affairs of God's people today.

I have been to the backside of the mountain a few times in my lifetime. On those occasions, God seemed to be absent, although I knew Him personally and intimately.

Those were moments when I felt spiritually empty, going through the motions. Looking back, often, I was angry with God and blaming Him for my predicament.

But, I could never remain angry with God. Nor could I quit serving Him. It occurred to me, I was the one in error, not Him, and I needed to repent and return to Him.

Others have experienced disappointment, loss, or trauma causing them to rethink God's goodness, His faithfulness, or providence—briefly, indefinitely, or sometimes permanently.

We should not be so quick to abandon our faith in the Lord during tough times. Instead, our intent should be to "*lean into Him*" even more.

One morning, before dawn, Jesus came to His Twelve Disciples walking on water. Impetuous Peter asked the Lord if he could accompany Him on the water. The Lord invited Peter, and all was going supernaturally well. Peter was walking on the water with his eyes fixed on the Lord.

Soon, however, the howling wind and turbulent water distracted him. Then as Peter took his eyes off Jesus, he sank. Yet, he had the "presence of mind" to call upon the Lord for help and safety.

Jesus rescued him immediately by pulling him out of the roaring waves. Once they were onboard the ship with the other Disciples, the wind stopped, and they all were safe (Matthew 14:25–32).

We, too, can become distracted as well. But as Peter demonstrated, we should also have the mind to fix our eyes on Jesus and call out to Him for rescue. Proverbs 20:22 tells us we can face our problems with faith in the Lord because He will deliver us.

God has given us prayer and His Word to sustain us in our times of distress, to comfort us, and to help build (or rebuild) our faith in Him.

Prayer

Through prayer, we communicate with God by expressing our affection and gratitude, concerns and fears, our needs and wants, our obstacles and afflictions, and our disasters and emergencies to the Lord. He is anxiously waiting to hear from us—and to help us.

Through prayer, we can revisit that state of perfect fellowship we had with Him in the beginning. It also allows us to follow His desires and obey His wishes. In addition, we can share all our love, joys, sorrows, and victories with Him who cares for us.

Here is what His Word says about our need for prayer and His desire to help us,

- Psalm 5:3 (NIV), "In the morning, LORD, you hear my voice; in the morning I lay my requests before you and wait expectantly."

- Psalm 27:13–14 (AKJV), "I had fainted, unless I had believed to see the goodness of the LORD in the land of the living. Wait on the LORD: be of good courage, and he shall strengthen thine heart: wait, I say, on the LORD."

- Luke 18:1 (NIV), "Then Jesus told his disciples a parable to show them that they should always pray and not give up."

- Philippians 4:6–7 (NIV), "Do not be anxious about anything, but in every situation, by prayer and petition, with thanksgiving, present your requests to God. And the peace of God, which transcends all understanding, will guard your hearts and your minds in Christ Jesus."

- Philippians 4:19 (AKJV), "But my God shall supply all your need according to his riches in glory by Christ Jesus."

- 1 Thessalonians 5:17 (AKJV), "Pray without ceasing."

- Hebrews 4:16 (AKJV), "Let us therefore come boldly unto the throne of grace, that we may obtain mercy, and find grace to help in time of need."

- 1 Peter 5:7 (AKJV), "Casting all your care upon him; for he careth for you."

Prayer is critical to our spiritual growth and vitality. As we pray, we find peace and joy as we enter into the presence of our loving Creator and Redeemer,

> It is the discipline of prayer itself that brings us into the deepest and highest work of the human spirit. Real prayer is life creating and life-changing. To pray is to change. Prayer is the central avenue God uses to transform us. If we are unwilling to change, we will abandon prayer as a noticeable characteristic of our lives. The closer we come to the heart beat of God the more we see our need and the more we desire to be conformed to Christ. In prayer, real prayer, we begin to think after God's thoughts after Him: to desire

the things He desires, to love the things He loves. Progressively we are taught to see things from His point of view. All who have walked with God have viewed prayer as the main business of their lives.[1]

God knows what we need before we ask Him for it, and He wants us to seek Him first (Matthew 6:32–33).

Urgent moments in our lives can produce deep, spiritual yearnings our words fail to express adequately. The Holy Spirit intercedes for us to express our urgent needs, wants, and desires to the Lord on our behalf (Romans 8:26).

Sometimes when our prayers go unanswered, we rethink our faith in God. Yet, there may be valid hindrances to unanswered prayer we can easily overlook.

One hindrance is how we view God. We see Him not as the almighty and all-knowing Creator and Sustainer, but as a puppet on a string whose sole purpose is to do our bidding like a genie in a magic lamp.

Such prayer is ineffective because the Lord will do exactly what He will do at the precise moment and in the precise manner that suits Him, not us. To us, His ways may appear to be strange at times, but they are always perfect because He always knows what is best for us in every situation.

Another hindrance is when we base our prayers on our ever-changing feelings. When we feel liked, accepted, prospering, and good about our circumstances, and ourselves God is with us, and all is good.

This line of thinking is flawed because it does not consider how many things including the Enemy, our own pride, selfishness, emotional wounds, sinful cravings, and even well-meaning people can influence our feelings to deceive us.

We must always remember our Lord is faithful always, and He is working on our behalf regardless of how we feel.

Another hindrance to prayer is poor or ungodly motives,

> You want what you don't have, so you scheme and kill to get it. You are jealous of what others have, but you can't get it, so you fight and wage war to take it away from them. Yet you don't have what you want because you don't ask God for it. And even when you ask, you don't get it because your motives are all wrong—you want only what will give you pleasure (James 4:2–3 NLT).

Also, a poor attitude toward our spouse will hinder our prayers' effectiveness as well (1 Peter 3:7). Yet, when my prayers were unanswered, my harbored pride and anger were often the culprits.

God never promised to give us everything we want or think we need. He always has a far better perspective than ours, and He will do for us and give to us what is best in every situation.

In Matthew 7:11, Jesus related how our ability to give good things to our children as parents is far surpassed by God's ability to provide what is good for us. Here, we will not give our children those things that are dangerous or unhealthy.

For instance, our child might ask to go somewhere or do something unsafe, or our teenager might ask for a new car or permission to stay out late with friends. From their perspective, they are certain what they are asking is safe or in their best interest. However, as loving parents, we will have a far better understanding of what is best and will respond appropriately.

Similarly, God has a better view of what is best for us. His perspective is eternal and omniscient, and His thoughts are transcendent and flawless. With goodness and mercy, He responds in our best interest every time.

Although we will never receive everything we ask for, yet God assures us He will supply all our needs while giving us those things that allow us to accomplish His perfect will through our exclusive, everlasting loving relationship He desires for us,

> See how very much our Father loves us, for he calls us his children, and that is what we are! But the people who belong to this world don't recognize that we are God's children because they don't know him. Dear friends, we are already God's children, but he has not yet shown us what we will be like when Christ appears. But we do know that we will be like him, for we will see him as he really is (1 John 3:1–2 NLT).

In times of uncertainty and panic, when we call on the Lord, He will hear our cries for help,

> I will call upon the LORD, who is worthy to be praised: so shall I be saved from mine enemies…In my distress I called upon the LORD, and cried unto my God: he heard my voice out of his temple, and my cry came before him, even into his ears…The LORD liveth; and blessed be my rock; and let the God of my salvation be exalted (Psalm 18:3, 6, 46 AKJV).

Ultimately, with the right motives and temperament (i.e., sincere, humble, reverent, selfless, Christ-centered, and God-honoring), we can pray with confidence knowing He hears us.

As we seek His Kingdom and righteousness first, we can experience His eternal peace, comfort, and joy as He supplies what we need (Matthew 6:33). Because He's promised to keep us to the end, we can rest assured the Creator and Sustainer of the heavens and the earth will keep His word also.

The Word of God

The Word of God (Bible) is a remarkable work. There is no other book like it anywhere. In over three thousand years of recorded human history, its promises and admonitions remain trustworthy and faithful. Psalm 12:6 (AKJV) tells us,

> The words of the LORD are pure words: as silver tried in a furnace of earth, purified seven times.

Earlier I related how my remarkable parents introduced me to the Lord and encouraged my spiritual growth and moral development.

Often, we shared about our Christian faith journey, and we talked about our favorite Bible passages.

The AKJV passage that resonated in Dad's heart the most emphasized the beauty, wisdom, and practicality of the Scriptures,

> The law of the LORD is perfect, converting the soul: the testimony of the LORD is sure, making wise the simple. The statutes of the LORD are right, rejoicing the heart: the commandment of the LORD is pure, enlightening the eyes. The fear of the LORD is clean, enduring for ever: the

judgments of the LORD are true and righteous altogether. More to be desired are they than gold, yea, than much fine gold: sweeter also than honey and the honeycomb (Psalm 19:7-10 AKJV).

As we grow more familiar with the truths and promises of the Bible, the Holy Spirit gives us biblical promptings to help us navigate life's uncertainties successfully.

We are the living proof of God's marvelous plan of redemption, whereby Jesus Christ reigns in us as Savior and Lord.

We authenticate our faith in God by His Word and the person of Christ. Both of these revelations deserve our reverent consideration,

> Two great revelations stand at the center of historic Christianity: the personal revelation of God in Christ and the propositional revelation of God in the Scriptures. The Christian claims that God has disclosed Himself in the Scriptures and in the Savior, in the written Word and in the Living Word of God. The evidence that the Bible is the written Word of God is anchored in the authority of Jesus Christ.[2]

We can find comfort in knowing Jesus Christ authenticates the Bible because He is the most important person in human history,

> By any and all standards Jesus Christ has always been regarded as the greatest figure in human history. On any list of the world's greatest men we always find at its head Jesus of Nazareth. Regardless of whether or not men acknowledge him as Savior and Lord they must pay tribute to Him as the world's outstanding man.[3]

The Bible is our perfect guide to living in the New Testament Age. As we read, study, memorize, and apply its principles to our lives, we grow into His productive people of faith and grace

Then, we become expressions of Christ's prophetic role by filtering everything we think, say, and do through a Bible-based perspective. In other words, we are people of the Bible who abide by its principles.

Although we may listen to secular experts for advice, the Word of God is the lamp and light to our footpath.

Faithful meditation on its precepts will discourage alienation from God while aiding us in resisting the habitual practice of sin (Psalm 119:11, 104–105).

In the twenty-first-century, more than ever, we need specialized knowledge and skill to be considered competent in our profession. Physicians study medicine, attorneys study law.

Likewise, we study the Word of God to be competent practitioners of the Christian faith.

We are spiritual beings, and our existence depends on Jesus Christ, the Living Word of God. He became flesh and lived among us (John 1:14). From His Word, God gives us the life-giving resources that help us to grow spiritually and morally, because His words are spirit and life (John 6:63).

Thus, the Bible is a holy book that we cannot read casually as we would a newspaper or novel. Instead, God must provide us with the spiritual insight to interpret and apply it correctly under the guidance of spiritually mature Christians who can teach the Bible *exegetically*.[4] Then, we "read out" of the Bible God's instruction for our lives and grow spiritually.

Even after the dust settles, the Lord can use us mightily to provide answers to questions and problems posed by our ever-seeking world.

With His Spirit, prayer, and His Word, we can inspire and transform a world in need of spiritual refurbishing.

Notes

[1] Richard J. Foster, *Celebration of Discipline, The Path to Spiritual Growth*, (San Francisco: Harper & Row, 1978) 30.

[2] Norman L Geisler, *Christian Apologetics*, 5th ed., (Grand Rapids: Baker Book House, 1991) 353.

[3] H.I. Hester, *The Heart of the New Testament*, 35th ed., (Nashville: Broadman Press, 1981) 5.

[4] *Eisegesis* is the antithesis of exegesis (or correct Bible study). It occurs when foolish conjecture from our selfish motives is imposed on the Bible. Destructive faith ensues whenever we *"read into"* the Bible false doctrines that cause confusion, doubt, and speculation.

Epilogue

Epilogue
Who Will Tell His Story?

Tell it Right!

The Lord Jesus Christ calls us to follow Him along  a glorious path of forgiveness, freedom, and fullness of joy. What lies ahead is often hidden or obscure. But that's ok because, as Proverbs 25:2 (NLT) tells us, "It is God's privilege to conceal things."

Yet, there is great comfort in knowing the Lord is with us each day to guide us throughout our earthly pilgrimage. He promises us in Matthew 28:20 (NLT), "And be sure of this: I am with you always, even to the end of the age."

Philippians 4:4 tells us to "rejoice in the Lord always." This is a special gift from God, provided and sustained by His Holy Spirit.

Herein also lies our power to tell His story—*right!*

We are to share His timeless message of love, faith, and redemption with a dying world searching for answers. Yet, we are responsible for telling it properly—*by living it faithfully!*

Early in my Christian life, I recognized we are not to take our Christian faith lightly due to its extremely high cost,

> Such grace is costly because it calls us to follow, it is a grace because it calls us to follow Jesus Christ. It is costly because it costs a man his life, and it is grace because it gives a man the only true life. It is costly because it condemns sin, and grace because it justifies the sinner. Above all, it is costly because it costs God the life of His Son: "ye were bought with a price," and what has cost God much cannot be cheap for us.[1]

Once, a pastor challenged me to use my mind constructively for the Kingdom, which ultimately begged this question, "If we were to give ourselves to the Lord completely, living according to the Bible, and trusting Him to fulfill His wonderful promises—*what could happen?*"

Trying to answer this question brought about many life-changing experiences for my family and me over the years as we sought to serve Christ.

For the answer implies we should no longer depend on our abilities and enterprises exclusively. Now, Christ is the center of everything, and we depend on Him exclusively.

But isn't this how we as Christians are supposed to live anyway? Proverbs 16:9 (NLT) tells us, "We can make our plans, but the LORD determines our steps." Moreover, Psalm 37:23 tells us our steps are "ordered" by the Lord, who takes delight in every step we take.

Answering the question means our self-centered, self-glorifying plans, goals, and objectives are "out the window," since they must be Christ-centered, God-honoring, and Bible-based,

> The Bible teaches us to make no distinction between secular and sacred in the world, work, and life. To understand and follow the calling of God is to know and do His good, pleasing, and perfect will. It is to live by biblical priorities. It is to find in Christianity a circle big enough to embrace all of life and give it meaning, purpose, and direction.[2]

Our thoughts, words, and actions will have to be filtered through a secondary question, "Will what I'm thinking, saying, or doing in at this moment help point someone to Christ?"

For me, over the years, that second question has been answered both yes, and no.

However, at this phase in my life, I want to finish well in furthering the Kingdom by living out the principles of Psalm 92:14 (AKJV), "They shall still bring forth fruit in old age; they shall be fat and flourishing."

I will never "arrive" and experience spiritual and moral completion in this life. I am still learning and growing. Yet, I have a wonderful example in Christ, who pledges His support and Spirit-power enabling us to serve Him.

Even more today, I am amazed at how the Lord is all-sufficient in supplying things beyond my control—especially, how He protects, provides, and guides me at the precise instant and in the precise way I need Him. The more I live, the more I experience His divine truth, "For all the promises of God in Him are Yes, and in Him Amen, to the glory of God through us" (2 Corinthians 1:20 NKJV).

Once a financial problem was so overwhelming, it precipitated my intense worry, followed by a panic attack. Although, I knew the Lord was with me, my fear of the unknown was too much for me to process effectively.

Then, out of the blue, a pastor friend contacted me and said he was praying for me. Then, he shared a Bible passage I have not since forgotten,

> Fear thou not; for I am with thee: be not dismayed; for I am thy God: I will strengthen thee; yea, I will help thee; yea, I will uphold thee with the right hand of my righteousness (Isaiah 41:10 AKJV).

At that moment, I realized the Lord is with me, and He is watching over me—even when I am not consciously aware of His presence (and providence). The financial problem was soon, and I must add, miraculously resolved.

Since that paradigm shift in my spiritual and emotional life, I have been astounded by how the Lord continues to "show Himself strong" in my life (2 Chronicles 16:9), especially during those times when I feel so very weak.

I deserve God's wrath and condemnation. None of my works for the Lord engender boasting since they are merely what He expects of me,

> "When a servant comes in from plowing or taking care of sheep, does his master say, 'Come in and eat with me'? No, he says, 'Prepare my meal, put on your apron, and serve me while I eat. Then you can eat later.' And does the master thank the servant for doing what he was told to do? Of course not. In the same way, when you obey me you should say, 'We are unworthy servants who have simply done our duty'" (Luke 17:7–10 NLT).

Yet, the Lord lavishly provides me with His forgiveness, freedom, and joy. I can never be "good enough" to earn His consideration. But I can continue pressing toward the heavenly prize He has in store for all those who love His appearing (Philippians 3:14, 2 Timothy 4:8). This is all He requires from us all.

Ultimately, my life has not been a bed of roses, but it has been exceptional nonetheless. Although the "outer house" continues to decay, the "inner man" is renewing daily (2 Corinthians 4:16). And for this, I am eternally grateful.

What a Wonderful Savior!

When I ponder my Christian journey, there is an old familiar hymn that expresses my adoration and gratitude for the Lord's providence and faithfulness over the years,

I Heard the Voice of Jesus Say[3]
Horatius Bonar
(1808—1889)

I heard the voice of Jesus say, "Come unto Me, and rest; Lay down, thou weary one, lay down Thy head upon My breast." I came to Jesus as I was, Weary and worn and sad; I found in Him a resting place, And He has made me glad.

I heard the voice of Jesus say, "Behold, I freely give The living water thirsty one, Stoop down, and drink, and live." I came to Jesus, and I drank of that life-giving stream; My thirst was quenched, my soul revived, And now I live in Him.

I heard the voice of Jesus say, "I am this dark world's Light; Look unto Me, thy morn shall rise, And all thy day be bright." I looked to Jesus, and I found In Him my Star, my Sun; And in that Light of life I'll walk Till trav 'ling days are done.

Notes

[1] Dietrich Bonhoeffer, *The Cost of Discipleship*, reprint, (New York: Simon & Schuster, 1995) 45.

[2] Patrick M. Morley, *The Rest of Your Life, a Road Map for Christians Who Want a Deeper Understanding of What to Believe and How to Live It*, reprint, (Grand Rapids: Zondervan, 1998), 196.

[3] Horatius Bonar, "I Heard the Voice of Jesus Say," *101 Hymn Stories*, Kenneth Osbeck, ed., (Grand Rapids: Kregel, 1982) 103.

About the Author

Floyd Bland has given his life to serving the Lord Jesus Christ as a pastor, teacher, ministry leader and administrator. He serves within his local church and for Not Of The World Ministries, Inc.

Floyd continues to help strengthen others in their faith in the Lord and in their relations with others by offering sound, practical, Bible-based interactive models for Christian living.

Floyd's other publications include: *The Christian Heritage: God's Answers for a Searching World, Radical Forgiveness Through the Eyes of Jesus,* and *Five Things Every Christian Must Know.*

Floyd completed his bachelor's degree at the California Baptist University, his master's degree at the American Baptist Seminary of the West, and his doctorate degree at the Pacific School of Religion.

For more than forty years, Floyd has been married to his best friend and helpmate, and together they have two grown children and a grandson.

www.ingramcontent.com/pod-product-compliance
Lightning Source LLC
Chambersburg PA
CBHW031126080526
44587CB00011B/1125